Your
New
Beginning

Your
New
Beginning

By

Dr. Sammy O. Joseph

Pulse Publishing House

© 1st edition 2016 Sammy O. Joseph

© 2nd edition 2017 Sammy O. Joseph

Published in the United Kingdom by
Pulse Publishing House
Box 15129
Birmingham
England
B45 5DJ

pulsepublishinghouse@harvestways.org

Bible quotes are from the King James Version of the Bible unless otherwise
stated.

Amplified quotes are from the Amplified Bible, © copyright 1995 by The
Zondervan Corporation and The Lockman Foundation.

Cover design and typesetting by Pulse Publishing House, England.

Printed in the United Kingdom by PULSE Publishing House

ISBN 978-0-9567298-8-0

Contents

Dedication

First and foremost, I dedicate this piece of writing to the Spirit of God; the Spirit of Truth without Whose divine enablement we who are called into the ministry would be essentially bare, barren and unfruitful – for without Him, we can do nothing!

Second, to the bravery of a widow who upon hearing the whispered instruction of the same Holy Spirit from the inspired lips of a foreign conference-speaker had conceived strength to birth the vision of *New Beginning Ministries – A Point of Hope*; a ministry wholly dedicated to solving the endemic problem of homelessness (and its related causes) in the city of Chatham-Kent, Ontario, Canada: Tracey Shavers.

Third, to my five *quivers* – Gabriella, David, Daniel, Priscilla and *our* dear Apostle Paul – my ministry gifts. I appreciate your tremendous support of me in the ministry and your release of me to go wherever I am sent of the Lord to minister His grace.

Finally, to you my reader. I pray you also will be able to hear the soft whispers of God's Spirit from the pages of this little booklet – and conceive in your mind, His vision of *your* very new beginning!

Chapter 1

Obey that Still, Small Voice

"Behold, to obey is better than sacrifice, and to hearken, than the fat of rams ..."

— Prophet Samuel

I had earlier been to Canada purposely on a fact-finding, familiarization tour in 2013. At that time, all I knew the Lord had instructed me to do was to *"Set your eyes, westward!"* In the *fall* of 2014 in Birmingham, England; He had unequivocally confirmed that He was ready to take our local *Experience HarvestWays Conference*, internationally. This was how the Holy Spirit had ordained my itinerary to Harrow, Ontario, Canada during Easter 2015 celebration. Here, we had conducted the first ever edition of *International Experience Harvestways Conference* in a church in Harrow. (Presently, I am writing extensively on the major highlights of this advent and outpouring of the Holy Spirit in my new, soon-to-be-released book *On Fire!* so I wouldn't be duplicating materials in this.)

Anyway, I had met Tracey Shavers at this conference. She had been invited by Mrs. Lee-Anne Frazer, the Canadian Regional Coordinator of the American *Break the Grey Ministries*. They both had attended our meeting in the company of a few of other friends.

We were not many at this gathering – but the Holy Spirit's impact on all had been riveting!

This tour had taken me to the southernmost tip of Canada in Windsor onto the Ambassador Bridge upon which I'd been driven into Detroit in Michigan, USA. I had reported at the *Total Christian Television* network studios in Detroit, ready to preach live, to over 100 million souls across North America: Canada and the United States. This was by far my largest- ever television audience. I know greater works will the Lord do through our ministries because He said so. In fact, a prophetess had confirmed His word unto me as she had prophesied during our conference at my host's church in Harrow:

> *"The Lord has opened the doors of ministry unto you in the Carolinas and Texas, USA and the cities of Toronto and Ottawa in Canada – as well as '100 Huntley Street' and the TBN television networks!"*

I look forward to the fulfilment of each of these words beginning with *you!*

Meanwhile, as we had completed the conference April 6th, 2015 with a *Ministerial Leadership Seminar*, participant-ministers from various other denominations and ministries had gracefully interceded for the local churches and ministries in the region along with my family; followed by the *Sammy Joseph Ministries*, the vision – and I.

It had been deeply a poignant time for me, personally speaking. I had come to Canada as a vessel of God's grace – and having being received as such had reciprocally warmed my heart. I had made new friends and forged deeper spiritual alliances. Now, it had been time to depart. (Sometimes, I encounter an inner pain at the conclusions of wonderful meetings as this. Gratefully, I have a family to return to – and a ministry to do, back home until another outreach opportunity beckons!)

Up until now, our ministries had *not* often received an honorarium. However, both my host church in Harrow, Ontario and the *International Gospel Deliverance Church* – across the Detroit River – in Southfield, Michigan, USA had offered their appreciations. The former had dipped into their offering basket's general collections, taken an envelope, sealed it and offered it to me. The latter had called for a "prophetic offering". Anyone who had thought they had a need for a prophetic encounter had willingly *'come forward for a word of the Lord from the mouth of the prophet'*. I had spoken the exact words Heaven had put on my lips for each! (Now, I must be quick to add here that this American mode of service, desiring 'a word of the Lord from the mouth of a prophet' had been totally alien to me. So also had been the warmth and eager expectation on the people's faces. These sharply contrast with the quiet, 'can-hear-a-pin-drop' worship services back in England). Of the thirty-something people who had placed a demand on God's anointing upon my life that evening, they *all* had confirmed every prophetic utterance had been perfectly accurate – yet I had had no prior knowledge of *any* of their private circumstances. Three-hundred U.S dollars had been taken in prophetic offerings. I had received the envelope handed over to me by Apostle (Dr.) Prince Miles; given thanks – and obeyed the bidding of the Holy Spirit: *I'd sown* the honorarium in designated seed-apportionments! It was just the very right thing to do!

Meanwhile in Harrow as the *International Experience Harvest-Ways Conference* had concluded, Dr. Alden Taylor had handed me the white envelope which I presumed had contained an honorarium for me. Yet again, the Holy Spirit had informed me of its appropriate end. I never even proceeded to see its contents. I knew I'd clearly heard Him say: *"Designated towards the Conifer Tree Felling!"* Almost immediately, I'd repeated what I'd heard to both pastor-couple that had hosted our ministries. They had only further confirmed the accuracy of the voice of the sweet Holy Spirit: *"There were two conifers"* they had choroused, in awe; *"we cut down one – and trusted the Lord to find the right guy to cut the other!"*

Well, *the* right guy had been me: the Holy Spirit *had* found me! How rejoiceful I had been!

Other friends and ministers had hugged – and exchanged complimentary cards with one another, myself included. The elderly Rev. & Mrs. Richard Davies had a firm grasp of my right hand; they shook it ever so warmly in turns. (We had even posed for a snapshot together). They had told me the advent and summary of their ministries spanning close to fifty years in four or five minutes. Eventually, the aged servant of God had grabbed my right hand, laid his left hand on my shoulder and prophesied upon me.

Afterwards, a woman of God had offered to take me out to lunch – in the company of an older minister designated to chauffeur me for the day: Minister Rick Brockwick, an ex-US Marines and brother-in-law to the Senior Pastor. He'd chauffeured me upon those silver-shiny wheels of their red Caddy. (Now, that car was the smoothest *drive* I ever rode on in my forty-seven years of existence!) We were in the very friendly atmosphere of Windsor's *Applebees'* in no time.

Once justice had been meted to the meals at the *Applebees'*, our benefactor had removed from her coat lapel, a miniature, beautiful golden cross. She had decorated the left lapel of my greyish-blue jacket and said: *"The Holy Spirit instructed me to decorate you with this cross-lapel since you fight the battles of the Lord of Hosts! Wear it anywhere He may lead you!"*

I'd fought back the tears!

Before I could have uttered a word, she had narrated how she had debated whether or not to attend that final morning's session. She had *really* wanted to, but had lacked the means to even get gas pumped into her car. So she had prayed to the Lord to miraculously meet that crucial need if it was His perfect will for her to be at the meeting. And God had answered the prayer through a friend she had run into as she'd pursued her business that morning. That friend had gently pressed some amount of money into her hands. It had been just enough to pay her due bills for that week, pump gas – and get her to the church venue on time. She had deducted her tithe, paid our meals – and folded the rest in a crinkled white envelope. She had pressed that envelope into my right hand. I'd tried to back down accepting it – but she hadn't budged. *"This is the very remnant of the seed a friend had given me earlier today, man of God"* she had said; *"spend this on refreshment while you changed flights on your way back to England."* It wasn't until I'd arrived at Newark, New Jersey, that I'd discovered it had totaled $13 USD (thirteen dollars) which had been receipted, once it had entered into our ministries' books! (And now, in a simple act of obedience to the voice of the Holy Spirit, I have worn that cross emblem on my different coats' lapels *everywhere* I've been).

Finally at the conference in Harrow, there had been yet another lady of tremendous faith and obedience at the closing meeting of April 6th, who had *"wanted to have a personal word"* with me before we had advanced to the *Applebees'*. When I had given her audience, these unmistakable words had poured out from her heart:

> *"Thank you Dr. Joseph, for your obedience to come to Harrow, to hold this conference!*
>
> *I'm a widow – and since my husband's passing, my whole life had almost approached a standstill. There had been an idea the Lord had given me shortly before my husband's transition about addressing the problem of men's homelessness in Chatham and providing them with a shelter in a christian setting ... I have been sit-*

ting on it for some years now. However, today as you spoke, I heard the Lord ask me to ask Him to ignite in me a new passion and zeal for this vision.

Now, I am ready: I feel the power of the Lord on the inside of me – ready to do His will!"

Within the space of a month of intensely seeking the face of the Father, consultations had begun with the city's clergy, churches and ministries. Even Chatham city officials had had a waft of the air of this vision gently drift at their sensory nerves. *Canadian Television – Windsor* also had helped raise the awareness of same, interviewing Sister Shavers and some team members at *The New Beginning Ministries – Point of Hope* on the local news! An ember had been fanned to flame.

I am persuaded to believe beyond all reasonable doubt, this vision could only have been the physical demonstration of God in action! That's one of the reasons behind the conception of this booklet: to encourage you – *whoever* you are, *wherever* you are, *whatever* your circumstances – that you too can indeed have that sparkling, brand new beginning you so desire!

Chapter 2

Anyone Can Have a Bright New Beginning

"You are never too old to set another goal or to dream a new dream."

— Aristotle

Anyone can *want* a new beginning. You too can have a sparkling, bright, brand new beginning.

Desire backed by resulting positive action to change is the proof of the "want". In other words, a new beginning doesn't just show up. Success doesn't just arrive on anybody's laps; it only will arrive as a result of a deliberate, changed mindset.

Suppose you've circled the base of a treacherous, snow-capped mountain for so long, confused and not knowing the safest trail to follow in an attempt to reach its frozen summit. You then visited *the* only local hiking gift shop at its base where you sighted *the* map of various trails – published by a wealthy local, suggesting *the safest* trail on which to hike. You would be barmy – to say the least – to entertain a debate within you whether or not you should purchase that map. You would be way off the mark to have purchased it – and never had it opened to observe a thoughtful study!

The scenario described above had been the stalling base where close to three million Canaan-bound Israelis had been footlocked, by the foot of Mount Seir. They had trodden well-cut footpaths that had shone with such brilliance from any moonless night! The only problem? They had been circling the base of the mountain, round and round, encompassing it for such a long while – having ignored the God Who had miraculously broken Pharaoh's iron-grips from off their necks. But suddenly, God had spoken to Moses:

> *"You have compassed this mountain long enough: turn you northward"*

— Deuteronomy 2:3

And just in an instant, there had been clarity in everyone's mind toward a common purpose: *Advance Northward!*

As you read these printed words, I pray the God of grace to cause the spirit of your mind to be flooded with His light so you would see the plight that had held you captive for so long. The Bible says *"the entrance and unfolding of Your words give light; their unfolding gives understanding (discernment and comprehension) to the simple" (Psalms 119:130; Amplified Version - my emphasis).*

Reception of the WORD

Notice my emphasis of that word *"gives"* in that scriptural reference. It is rendered in the present continuous form — "gives". That means whenever or wherever occurs the reception of the words of the Lord into *a* human spirit, there is illumination. According to the Amplified Version's rendition of that verse, there must additionally be unfolding, discernment and comprehension. In other words, the souls of the recipients are forever altered, for the best!

Not only this, if a person was un-regenerated, for instance, and a good balanced preaching of the Word is received into their inward being; the spirit of that fellow will become quickened. Re-generated. Alive. Such will become alive towards God's Spirit – and become fanned by the *ruach;* that is the very breath of God. This exactly is what happens when we say a person has become "Born Again." Born anew. Born of God's Holy Spirit. Such a person can now see him / herself in the light of God's perspectives. It now all of a sudden makes all the sense in the world to a person in prison, for instance, the gravity of their crime: They become overwhelmed. For the first time in many years, they may even cry, experiencing true remorse for their crime, indicative of their inner feelings! What the law-enforcement, the judiciary and the correctional institute attempted in vain to make them realize suddenly becomes pristine clear to their conscience.

On the other hand if another person, for instance already knew God when the engrafted word of God was received by them with meekness, such becomes renewed in their mind. This exercise in turn, has lasting positive effects on their life.

A lot of people there are walking, cycling and traveling about freely in the societies of the world today who indeed are helpless, hapless, clueless prisoners of their very own minds. They could be held captive by unforgiveness. Believe you me; if they continued to walk in unforgiveness, the Bible says that roots of bitterness would sure fester. When those roots have deepened in the soils of their hearts well enough, what associated physical manifestations that often result are incurable body-aliments, sicknesses and afflictions. I am sure you would probably have one or two people with whom you could easily associate this scenario; people who have passed life-imprisonment custodial sentences upon themselves because of their personal choices to *not* forgive and forebear grievance(s)!

Not only does the reception of the word of the Lord positively affect the human spirit, minds and bodies, it does also produce unspeakable, indescribable joy full of glory! That joy in turn generates tons of energy from the very depth of the receptive human souls. And wherever energy is generated, there will be no want of fire, heat, heating, melting – and so on and so forth. All these are somewhat by-products of the light of God's Word fanned into a fierce, fiery, fire within the chambers of the human spirit.

What chains can resist the billowing descent of the fire of the Holy Spirit?

There is none!

By this fire curses are broken; inherited and genealogical disturbances, vaporized. Have you ever seen an uncontainable forest fire in action? It razes down to ashes, anything in its pathway.

I am praying that the fire of God's Word will burn from within your heart today.

Let me bring this phenomenon of the Word producing light and fire closer home to you. Remember those close to three million emancipated, confused Jews at the foot of Mount Seir we earlier read of? They had become dejected, despondent, depressed, defensive and defeated; life's disappointments had diluted their resolve to inherit the promised land of Canaan. They were defenseless, weary – and worn out in their minds. But no sooner than Moses had received – and instructed them – God's word of command to "advance northward" had they experienced a renewed surge of life! Energy had suddenly resumed into the red blood cell corpuscles that coursed their veins. If there was anyone feeling that deadly, lethargic feeling caused by regrets and disappointments, disobedience and wasted opportunities; what such needed was a good, full dosage of the undiluted, incorruptible word of God which forevermore is alive *(1 Peter 1:23-25).* The Word will produce in them such a tremendous forceful surge in energy caused by God's light. This light in turn produces optimism, determination, and an inextinguishable strong, fiery passion to think, say and do what is right, always.

Isn't that phenomenal?

You Just Can't Mouth Change

You see, you need a determined, purposeful and an optimis-

12

tic heart whose passion is inextinguishable in order to conquer the summit of your quest: the new beginning! You just can't *mouth* change; you've got to have that inner strength and courage to really *want* to change.

Now, the truth is you will not possess an inextinguishable strength or determination to overcome for instance, the struggle with an addiction or a family history of curses by your self efforts. Only God's Holy Spirit can muster within you, such incomprehensible strength. But you have your very own part to play in the process too: willingness to imbibe the Word! Only then will you become unstoppable.

> *Thirsty for the Change;*
> *Hunger for the Word!*

Make that your mantra that births your new beginning! Master Jesus put it like this:

> *"Blessed are they which do hunger and thirst after righteousness: for they shall be filled."*

— Matthew 5:6

One Rural Shepherd-Boy with an Inextinguishable Passion

There was once a brilliant teenager by the name, David. He was a rural, shepherd-boy with a difference: he exuded so much an inextinguishable passion that his seven older half-brothers had him sidelined and relegated to the backside of the desert.

They tried to figure him out but they just couldn't. At the end, they just had to *have a reason to pin his banishment into the desert upon!* You see, David was the only mixed-child among the lot; a product of Jesse's sexual frivolity with an un-named Moabitess. The Ammonites and Moabites were two of the tribes God had commanded the children of Israel to *not* intermingle with; they were to be banished from the commonwealth and covenant of Israel even unto their four-hundredth year of genealogy (See *Deuteronomy 23:3-4).*

Moreover, young David who happened to be the last born of eight sons was precocious. To be precocious is to possess abilities and inclinations much farther ahead of one's young age or peers. In other word, he was way far ahead in knowledge, wisdom and understanding – farther advanced possibly than all his older brothers! It was thus very easy to excommunicate him from the family home to the rugged, dangerous, rough, lonely places in the backside of Bethlehem's desert.

Are you inhabiting the rugged, dangerous, rough, lonely places of life – feeling abandoned by friends, families or a loved one? David's story should somewhat be a recourse to your solace!

Some of David's Exceptional Innate Abilities

In every one of us, there's at least, an exceptional innate ability. It was God-created, God-designed and God-gifted. It is always residual, though; and that's the exact part you must 'desperately' desire to effect, to experience *your* new beginning! Do not let anyone talk you out of the truth that you are of inestimable value to God; *that exactly, the accuser or abuser would very much be intent on doing.* Jealous, envious and raging, bullies will feel intimidated by their perception of your gift. In effect, they will undoubtedly work hard to bring you down. Your acquiescence with this truth – that you're inherently gifted by the Creator – is your saving grace, anytime, anywhere, any day! By reading this booklet, you're now being both empowered and emboldened to take the 'fight' to your within – and at the same time encouraged to roll your sleeves and get ready to 'dig deeper' below the surface-soil of your very existence. Both the *recognition* and the *discovery* of your latent gifts are a tag-team ferocious weapon you must be ready to unleash in the face of life's trials, troubles, temptations and turmoil.

You *must* discover *your* innate abilities. And that by *yourself.* I alone must be the one to discover mine; it is right within my sole jurisdiction to do so. Discovering yours is rightly very much within your sole jurisdiction too; it is the very first step anyone takes towards their breakthrough!

When David had discovered his God-endowed gifting, he further had discovered the following:

- *His self-worth:*

The combination of the harshness of the attitudes of David's bigger, older brothers; a weak dad Jesse, and a self-discovering, emerging, daring, precocious ruddy-faced lad only spelt one word: Turmoil! The young guy just couldn't be bothered! He solaced his life of turmoil with a deeper sense of *the* self-discovery of his self-worth.

> *Blessed are a people who dare to self-reflect in abject solitude!*

For you who are afraid of aloneness, take a cue: Solitude is the only tool that will reveal unto you the true *you!* Solitude alone has the power – *if* rightly engaged – to either build you up or tear you down.

- *God's compassion and mercy:*

The shepherd-boy's discovery had been astounding. He had uncovered the mechanics of God's grace covenant. He had acquired the knowledge undergirding God's mercy and compassion freely made available, which, any sinner or accursed mixed-Moabite like himself could lay hold upon and be preserved to thrive thereupon. Such *an* understanding does *not* avail itself to a care-free mind; it only comes by the diligent understudy of that compassionate God Who longs to shower His mercy and compassion upon all who come to Him. His Word says: *"The Lord is gracious, and full of compassion; slow to anger and plenteous in mercy" (Psalms 145:8).*

- *His passion for music and the worship of God:*

This afflicted young man had further reached deeper into his soul to discover his ravishing passion for music and the worship of God. Many a time, people who are gifted in music and worship will be able to compose, arrange and produce masterpieces.

Furthermore, David had discovered his wittiness for inventing musical instruments, while in the desert. The same rugged woods of the forest had become his workshop for the invention of virtuoso, hand-crafted viol, lyre and other stringed instruments *(2 Chronicles 7:6).*

Doesn't this incorrigible young lad left abandoned to die beat your imagination?

- *His passion for the few sheep he was tending*:

Young shepherd boy David had also developed an unfathomable passion for the upkeep and well-being of the few ewes he was tending back-side of the desert.

Passion for those who seemed somewhat like the "weaker vessels" in life – or occupants of both the lower echelons of society and the despicable places of life is essential if we must become the instrument of a lasting change in others! This part of the curriculum, no university or theological seminary in the world would teach. Humility can only come by brokenness.

- *He had developed a sense of sustainable economic growth*:

Very soon, he was bottling and supplying milk, fermented cheese – and other dairy products from his farm of a flock of a few sheep to the adjacent villages! The young man had developed a sense of sustainable economic growth so much that he had happily sacrificed his very dear life in order to save that of an ewe or a lamb either when the bear or the lion had posed predatory threats. Predatory threats to any of his livestock had been well translated to mean a threat on his financial investments!

- *He had also invented and carved an innocuous offensive weapon: the sling!*

David not only had developed sharp business acumen, he had also invented and carved an innocuous offensive weapon: the sling! He had been notorious with his sling and the leather-pouch that had held the stones. All bye-passer travelers, and neighboring peasants had described him by his appearance: *The-Shepherd-boy-With-The-Sling-And-Leather-Pouch-Slung-Across-Chest*. Wow, what an unmistakable young man! Much

17

like Prophet Elijah had had a distinctive appearance that had marked him differentiated from his closest peers!

David also had so much faith in God, himself and his witty inventions. Whenever he had maneuvered those crude inventions into positions in order to practise and sharpen his skills, charged anointed atmosphere had been induced. Imagine, for instance, when he had laid his hands on the flute or the lyre to play, all the birds had chirped along to his tune. Weird happenings had occurred. Possibly the hyenas too had howled farther away in the distant mountains in the night as he had strung the strings of the lyre – and sang in the pitch-dark, star-studded sky. Can you imagine that? But that in reality could well have been the case, because of the presence of God's anointing upon him. You see, anywhere the anointing is present; there miracles attest.

- *He had cultivated and developed his mind's power of focus:*

This young lad had so much unleashed ferocious attacks upon his intended targets in the solitude and secrecy the desert had offered him until he had become a sharp-shooter! A marksman you can't afford to mess with. Such is the power of focus. You couldn't dissuade him from his conviction and trust in his crude and ornate assault weapons: a simple wooden sling, some stones and a sling-purse!

That was it!

That was all he ever would need in a few years' time to put the defiant giant Goliath from Gath of the Philistines to an eternal sleep.

At this juncture, I would ask you: *"Do you really desire a brand new beginning?"*

If you answered in the affirmative; then, begin a soul-search to discover your innate abilities and harness your misfortunes, prevailing desert condition, solitude or hardship into sharp-shooting opportunities by frequent practice because of a solid self-belief!

Chapter 3

Truths are Truer than Facts

"Let God be true but every man a liar."

— Apostle Paul

Not only does everyone have innate qualities within them that can *only* be brought onto the surface by deep soul-searching, every human on this planet earth has a unique date with destiny. Unfortunately, many don't realize that truth. It is a truth – because truths are higher – and much truer than facts!

Most children have an average of between fifteen and twenty years of basic formal education, *if* they opt for that route to self-sustenance. What everyone learns in that time-frame are plainly facts; facts and figures that are necessary to enable them function in an educated world! But you and I know that not all folk who possess a first or second degree do function well in real life! Sometimes, there are some *Bachelors, Masters, Ph.D* and *Professorial* degree holders that can't seem to possess the basic understanding of how to get a firm hold on *life* itself!

How could that be? It is because no academician is empowered to impart you the TRUTH. What investment your thousands of hard-earned cash, state or university loan procured you is a formidable formal university degree.

Definitely, a formal education is important to give you a worthy foothold on your career ladder in this physical world. I possess my degrees too – and they are a blessing because they open doors to different spheres of life. So you can see that I am not trying to knock formal education. No, not at all. What I am trying to pass across is that laudable as your formal education and pedigree of scholastic aptitude may be, none of those degrees can *move* a single devil! Neither rhetoric, theatrics – nor 'theoretics' move Satan! Let me say it more succinctly: Years in formal education or indeed any secular apprenticeships do not cast out a demon, heal an incurable disease – or indeed give anyone immense authority to foreclose an impending disaster. Only the received truth of God's word empowers. Inspires. Saves. Delivers – and delivers, absolutely!

Today, you may be in a hard place; but I have a word from Heaven *just* for you: You're being built up for a date with destiny. On that day – that is soon fast approaching – you would look back on your frivolous and rebellious pathways and *then* realize that the "setbacks" suffered, are indeed preparatory steps to your "set-up's". I hope you do have the capacity to receive and respond to this truth! Because the moment you encounter the prophetic – a truly, anointed prophetic; light from Heaven shines on your dark places. Your mind becomes illuminated and enlightened. Some four-hundred men experienced this type of glorious illumination I am describing here. They soon mushroomed into six-hundred. Their minds' lightbulbs had suddenly lit – and had kept lighting others! They had had a unique encounter with the anointed, chosen, ordained vessel of God!

David's 400-Man-Army

You must have heard about the "Fortune-500" Group of companies but probably *not* "David's 400-man-army". Their story is told in *1 Samuel 22*. Anytime you have the opportunity, it would do you some good to check their story out. You're comparably better off than any of them, I dare say! Some of them were depressed, disgruntled, distressed and deep in debt. But they had met an anointed prophet of God; a near kinsman, David! He would train and raise them into a formidable army that would confront Israel's most dreaded perennial enemy: the Philistines. At the worst, they would fortify the strongholds against potential surprise attacks from Saul and his strong, well-rounded, 3 000-man chosen army.

As earlier hinted, David had understood that he would have *his* day; a specific date with destiny. He would surely become Israel's future king. Not only would he become Israel's future king, he had also maintained a tight rein on the age-long ordained but unrevealed truth that he belonged in the Messianic lineage; the lineage of Jesus Christ, the King of kings Who was to come through the ancestry of Judah's tribe.

"Oh, what a discovery", you sigh. But same fate awaits you. You also have a date with destiny. If you are born again, you additionally are spiritually engrafted into the glorious lineage of Jesus Christ, the King of kings and the Lord of lords!

What's In Your House?

Sometimes, an anointed person finds themselves in trouble through none of their doing at all; they are left destitute, like young David had been. If this happens, wisdom calls such a person to request:

- *What's in my house?*
- *What's in my hand?*
- *Who do I have, willing and available?*

You wouldn't be perceived as wise to run helter-skelter, rally horses and recruit horsemen to build a coalition of fighters in the day of battle. Read the synopsis of David's predicament in this story of this spectacular season in his life. His mode of operation begs for deployment in your current hardship:

"David therefore departed thence, and escaped to the cave Adullam: and when his brethren and all his father's house heard it, they went down thither to him.

And everyone that was in distress, and everyone that was in debt, and everyone that was discontented, gathered themselves unto him; and he became a captain over them: and they were with him about four hundred men.

And David went thence to Mizpeh of Moab: and he said unto the king of Moab, let my father and my mother, I pray thee, come forth, and be with you till I know what God would do for me.

And he brought them before the king of Moab: and they

dwelt with him all the while that David was in the hold."

— 1 Samuel 22:1-4

Some truths are undeniably evident about David from these five verses of scriptures:

- *He was a fugitive running from a potential assailant who had wanted to snuff out his light in thick obscurity: Saul and the army of Israel;*
- *He loved and honored both his parents even in his predicament. He realized in time they had to be kept beyond the borders of Israel. (It was only naturally logical that the only country he could hide them in was Moab – because his mom was a national);*
- *He required to gather and train an army of his own – most of whom were societal misfits and rejects.*

No Exemptions

There are no exemptions to who can become overwhelmed! Even anointed people can soon be overwhelmed by life's challenges, *if* perfect care is not taken. I'm pretty sure you know that, by now: Anointed people can be surrounded by so much turmoil that living just ordinary day-to-day, basic life, becomes a challenge.

For some, their challenges are economical. Bills mount up – and become unpaid! That leads to a court action – or a Judge's enforcement ruling. Bailiffs are soon on the hunt; an eviction, looms. The anointed comes under attack. He or she could be rendered homeless. This is just a possible scenario.

Another basic, day-to-day, living tug-of-war could be the emotional anguish caused by the betrayal of an unfaithful spouse: the innocent party is suddenly exposed with no option of a place to run and hide. There could be a dozen of scenarios I could count off of my fingertips from a repertoire of experiences I have gathered from nearly three decades of counseling in ministry!

Some other times though, a young person inherits troubles like young David had from the frivolity of his parents. (I'd preached from the backdrop of the Moabites' curse at my first live-telecast on *TCT TV - WDWO* Detroit, April 2, 2015 titled "Barrier Breakers"). Truth is, there is nothing academic excellence could do to remove the tarnish of an inherited trouble. Medical sciences may proffer suggestions – but no scientist up until today has ever found the permutation to manufacture hemoglobin or indeed the red blood cells of *any* human. And they will never be able to. This is one arena to which I always point out the outlandish supremacy of the Creator God above all else.

You see, no spiritual inherited troubles could be sliced, diced or *lasered* away. Only the anointing in the name of Jesus Christ of Nazareth does reverse and heal such troubles.

Alcohol-abuse tendencies, for instance, have been found to be passable onto a fetus in the womb of a pregnant mother. So also could nicotine in cigarettes could be passed onward through active, passive or recessive smoking. What of irremovable consequences in behavioral patterns that are prone to be inherent in a youngster through the inherited recessive genes of his or her fore-parents? How much calculus could you perform to differentiate that soul from their inherited psychological traits?

Apart from the *unexpected* and the *uncontrollable* factors discussed above that could play significantly on a person's emotional being, some other person may become busted, disgusted, depressed and disgruntled in life because of their doing. Their *personal irresponsibility*.

Some folk search and look for troubles – until they find some. Take for example someone who decides to join a street gang – and its gang culture on an initiation ceremony. Suppose on that very first day of their initiation, they had committed a capital punishment. They been apprehended – and arraigned before a judge. The judge had handed down a capital sentence.

Would that be smart on their part? I think not!

Take for another instance a married man who decided to gamble away family money at the casinos – and still expected to be loved and peaceably married. *Excuse me, are you serious?* Seriously?

What about a young adult who refused to come clean off drugs – and had had their 'loving' family kick them out onto the streets only for them to feel resentful and bitter against their family's 'tough love'!

You see, people who *want* better – the kind of new beginning that I have been writing about, come to *the place of surrender;* the place where they own total responsibility for their irresponsible actions. You simply cannot continue to live out this entitlement culture with all its trappings through deception, lie and vanity – and expect better!

Any person who aspires unto wholeness *must* first realize they're in a pretty bad shape – and request help to get straightened out. It's only then that help can be administered.

Such help too should be gratefully received.

You've probably heard the saying: "You can lead a horse to the stream but you can never force him to drink the water!" And that's exactly correct.

There's absolutely no need to continue to play *Hide – 'n – Seek* with your life: Realize you're in a pretty bad shape. Be humble enough to ask for help. Then receive the help offered! Notice what those four hundred men did: The Bible says they went *down* to David:

> *David therefore departed thence, and escaped to the cave Adullam: and when his brethren and all his father's house heard it, they went down thither to him.*

— 1 Samuel 22:1

Have you also noticed that rivers originate from mountains and hills – and *not* from valleys? So also it must be that when you're in the ditch, you *must* look up for help. That attitude of *looking up* tells of a humble, teachable heart willing to receive:

> *"I will lift up mine eyes unto the hills, from whence cometh my help. My help comes from the LORD, which made heaven and earth."*

— Psalms 121:1-2

Be humble. Receive that help that God is sending you. This booklet actually is a miniature help of God, unto you today.

Also, *David's* 400-man-army did *not* discriminate against one another. Bad is worse enough; it needs no comparisons. No one looked down at the other in the disheveled corps scheme and say: *"Hey you, I am better than you. I am indebted but not depressed!"* We know saying that would be a blatant lie; indebted people are worried people! But, no! No one belittled another. There was an unspoken understanding of mutual love and respect in the camp! Every man looked for his brother's interests; they each had another's back. Remember, they had same denominator-enemies: Saul and the Philistines?

Likewise, your new beginning will necessarily include people who are battling to overcome the same denominator-enemies. Say, for instance, an addiction, an illness an excess weight-loss or a pain. Platoon members drink from the same water-bottle without discrimination!

David may have inherited a weak, disgruntled, emotionally-unstable and indebted set of people as recruits; but in a little while, he had sent them onto a top-notch boot-camp. With the help of the Spirit of the Lord, they had emerged a pretty formidable army – much akin to the *U.S. Special Sea, Air and Land - SEAL teams!* These initial four-hundred men had become invincible and renowned. Beautiful young ladies had even caught their fancy, each. They had soon been wedded and procreated. Yes, that's what God can do: Turn destinies around, in an hundred-and-eighty-degree turn, in such a short while.

The abject of men in the city had suddenly become the salient subjects of discussions in the entire country. The unwanted had become the indispensable power-players. Isn't it written: *"The stone which the builders refused is become the head stone of the corner."* The Psalmist actually raised his fore-finger and pointed us all to He Who alone could accomplish such a feat. *"This is the Lord's doing; it is marvelous in our eyes" (Psalms 118:22-23).*

This is the type of 'turnaround' I envision in your very life, today!

Chapter 4

Live Your New Life with Ease

"We can ignore even pleasure. But pain insists upon being attended to. God whispers to us in our pleasures, speaks in our conscience, but shouts in our pains: it is his megaphone to rouse a deaf world."

— C.S. Lewis, *The Problem of Pain*

Are you really ready to *obey* the sweet, gentle voice of the Holy Spirit of God?

Do you really *desire* change?

Have you carefully *evaluated* your misfortunes – and discovered rare opportunities for a bright, brand new beginning?

Have you *unearthed your innate abilities?*

Are you of *a humble and lowly heart*?

If you answered all those questions affirmatively, then you shall indeed have that new beginning you so much have dreamed! Nothing in your past should becloud your vision. Neither should "the thief" be further permitted to steal from you. I do trust you recognize who he is? He is the devil, the wicked one whose main aim is to surreptitiously *"steal, kill and destroy"* (John 10:10). Neither ever again permit the waster of destinies to waste yours. (By the way, I also do trust you're aware who that is? It's not the devil; it's *you).* For only *you* could withstand the attainment of your destiny!

The prodigal son's proverbial story the Savior Jesus Christ had recounted to us had developed an interesting outcome when the outspent young man had simply paused to *reason with himself.* Jesus says, *"he came to himself" (Luke 15:17).* What a blessing to finally come to a place of self-examination. It sure sounds like the soul-searching I earlier mentioned. If it demands you quit the hustle and bustle of the city – and the going-on's in the hoods to go sit in the quiet of the woods to reason, then what prevents you?

The selfishness that undergirds every depression has to depart. Suicidal thoughts have to be conquered by the truth of God's Father love that you're loved; very much loved, indeed. Lonely, wafting thoughts have smothered the truth that you're *not* alone, for: *"Yea, though I walk through the valley of the shadow of death, I will fear no evil: for thou art with me; thy rod and staff they comfort me" (Psalms 23:4).*

You have no husband – and are scared you will be by yourself all the days of your life? That certainly couldn't be true except you let it be. Swap *your* perspective-glasses, will you? While you're pining away waiting for someone to approach you with love, there's certainly someone special destiny has assigned you to love!

Wouldn't it just be very fulfilling searching for such until you've found them?

Instead of entertaining fear of heading for the dusty shelves at forty, you certainly could foster or adopt a motherless baby into your world. You certainly could pour all your love into such a willing, receptive vessel, couldn't you? Love certainly doesn't have to be sexual if unmarried!

And for you *Mr. Toughie*, that mean spirit in you has to be evicted. *You* serve it an eviction notice, right now! Serve the quit notice on the retaliatory mindset that had got you nothing but chains, pains and no gains up until now! Wise people don't engage in every battle; they choose their battles wisely. That's why I am asking you to give your battles to the Lord. He says they're His to fight; not yours *(Romans 12:18-21)*.

Homeless? Make up your mind to kick those wicked habits and poor choices of the circles of friends you have made that have brought you this low! Re-train. Apply for a job. Get a job, no matter how lowly.

You may even start your own business from scratch without having to scratch your head. (I've informed you where to look: deep within you.) From that littleness, God will lift you high. But you possibly cannot continue to engage pettiness and low thoughts and think you'd become lofty and respectable. Gangs and ghetto-thoughts haven't got anything good to offer you all these past years – and you know it, they never will. So stop wasting away.

Addicted drug-user? Yes, you can overcome the addictions. All of David's 400-man-army were strictly addicts to what stuff had *got* them!

But do you know the Goodnews?

All of them had beaten their addictions. They'd come clean and straight – ready to walk the narrow road. They had been with themselves, soul-searched, accepted responsibility for their part in whatever had brought them so low. But they'd also taken it upon themselves to change. When they couldn't be able to kick their wasteful habits so easily, they by themselves had reasoned deep within themselves who to call for help.

They'd sought the anointing upon David's life.

Always, it's been the lower who had sought for the higher; that's the norm! You too must seek for the Most High God. *"For thus saith the LORD unto the house of Israel, Seek ye me and ye shall live" (Amos 5:4).*

When you're ready to live this new beginning life that I've been expounding to you, God will be found of you. He too is looking for you! He will direct your pathways to a godly shepherd after His Father heart to shepherd, nurture and train you in spiritual matters, for David was an experienced shepherd-boy!

In more than twenty-five years of ministering the Gospel, I have witnessed addicts quit the anger and the selfishness that had so eaten into them. They had become sober and responsible members of the society. There are surely godly shepherds dotted across the horizons of the lands that would help you achieve your new beginning!

If you're currently reading this from an incarceration unit, please make up your mind to *not* exit the penitentiary system "a half-baked bread" like Biblical Ephraim. Rather, aim at becoming a well nurtured, well-grounded individual. Someone well-baked by the Holy Spirit See *(Hosea 7:8)*. If however, you're awaiting the administration of the lethal injection, it still makes no difference to your fulfilling your vision of having a brand new beginning. *"To be absent from the body"* the Bible says, is to *"be present with the Lord"* (2 *Corinthians 5:8)*. You cannot afford to miss the promise of new and abundant life the Lord Jesus Christ promises in *John 10:10b*.

By the power of the Holy Spirit, I minister to you this day:

> You won't cave in under the pressure.

> Your Maker is strong – and so are you.

> Your model is both patented and indestructible.

> You're indomitable because the One Almighty God who created *your* spirit – Whom the scripture refers to as the *"Father of spirits"*, operates in irresistible power and authority!

When you become His child, all His authority becomes delegated upon you – whether you're in jail or in the city. Dare you by faith receive this promise from the Father, today?

Make this be your very new beginning.

If my message has been used by the Spirit of God to prompt – or answer – your quest for the bright, brand new beginning your heart always had yearned for, pray with me. Ask the Lord Jesus Christ into your heart, right away:

"Dear Lord Jesus,

I ask for my very new beginning.
I hereby do open the door of my
heart unto You. Please come in.
Forgive me my sins. Cleanse – and save me!
Write my name in the Book of Life.
Thank you so very much!

Amen!"

If you prayed that prayer from your heart by faith, you've become a child of God. Write me today to: *'reverendsammy@harvestways.org'*

OR

Sammy Joseph Ministries
Box 15129, Birmingham,
England, United Kingdom, B45 5DJ

I simply can't wait to read from you.

Congratulations!

Chapter 5

Now That You are Saved

"Desire the sincere milk of the word, that ye may grow thereby."

- Apostle Peter

Now that you're saved, let me quickly advise you of two or three mandatory, essential steps you *must* take to bolster you walk with the Lord:

1. *Pray in the name of Jesus.* Imagine having a key in your hands that opens a door. Prayer is the key to accessing God. It is talking to God through the only exalted name of the Lord Jesus Christ (*Acts 4:12*).

   Talking to Jesus doesn't need to be compli-cated any more than you talking to a friend is. Jesus Christ calls you, friend (*John 15:15*).

2. Pick up your Bible and start reading. The likely question that is going to agitate your mind is: *"What book can I start my reading from?"*

I have always advised people to start reading from the Gospel according to Saint John.

If you read two chapters a day: one in the morning and one in the evening before you sleep, you will be completing reading the entire Bible in two years!

3. Ask the Lord to connect you with a true, living Bible-believing church where you will integrate with other saints – and be taught the undiluted word of God so that you may grow *(1 Peter 2:23).*

Worship with Us

The Harvestways Int'l Church
(Birmingham, U.K.)
Holloway Hall
Northfield, Birmingham,
England, United Kingdom
B31 1TT
Sundays: 12 noon
Wednesdays: 8pm
Home Cell Friday Prayer Meeting: 7pm
Tel: (+44) 7758195466 / 7854675159
e-mail: admin@harvestways.org

**The Harvestways Int'l Church
(Nigeria)**

1 Harvest Way, Off Elewura Street
Behind Zartech / GLO Office,
Off Elewura Street
Challenge, Ibadan, Oyo State,
Nigeria, West Africa.
Sundays: 9am & Tuesdays: 6pm
e-mail: nigeria@harvestways.org

Other Books by the Author

Other books by the author are available at any Christian bookshop near you, *Pulse Publishing House* locations or from our website: *harvestways.org*

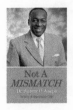

Not A Mismatch
Your adverse life experiences or circumstances do not make you irrelevant. No matter your background, color, ethnicity or creed, the Creator has your very name written in the palms of His hands – and calls you by that name. You are not a misfit. You are not mismatched against your challenges; strength yet avails for your emancipation (168 pages)

When the Chips Are DOWN
Based upon Jeremiah's observations in his elegiac poetic book of Lamentation, the author attempts to both depict the descriptions and manifested-traits of one whose chips are down! You will be enraptured by the way the author has deployed sheer literary genus and a sharp, enrapturing writing style to describe the intuitive bald eagle – how he triumphs over his gruesome molting season in the wild. Learn in this book, your very personalized "way of escape" provided by the loving Heavenly Father out of the feelings of despair, despondency, desolation and depression. (110 pages)

APPRECIABLE Gifts

Seekers in quest of attaining inner peace with the heavenly Father, deepening satisfaction in their friendships/relationships, healings from life's brokenness – enhancing their sexuality and marriages need search no further. Within the pages of *Appreciable Gifts* lie your missing trophies! Read and apply guideposts on the parameters of offering, accepting, cherishing, maintaining – and abounding in gifts! The messages therein will positi-vely impact your relationships for a lifetime! (183 pages)

DESTROYING the Power of DELAY

This book is an expository piece of work, written in a scriptural, thought-provoking style. The author aimed at sharing with you from more than twenty years of counseling in ministry, how to avoid the endearing long arms of delay; and if you're already entangled in a wild romance with the hated alien, the quickest way of escape from him. (220 pages)

GIDEON: Releasing the Potentials Within You

This book draws analogies from the life of Gideon (one of Israel's Judges) and applies them to how you can effectively release the hidden potentials within you. Written in easy, straightforward, simple language, you will find basic practical insights that will help lift you above common mediocrity levels in life! (176 pages)

Before You Step into Someone Else's Shoes

This book contains easy-to-do guides on how you will not repeat the costly mistakes made by others faced with a fresh opportunity to begin anew after suffering a heavy setback. We have also provided essential checklists to anyone willing to step into shoes ordained of God for them – as well as checkmating the mutineers! (46 pages)

Download *PULSE On-line*, freely at
www.harvestways.org

Become a *Sammy Joseph Ministries* Vision Partner

Our commitment is to:

- Pray – and cover you daily in prayers, that God's undeniable blessings be upon your you and your household.

- Keep ministering the Word of God diligently.

- Minister to you once a month via a telephone call from us.

- Minister to you in a personal newsletter from Dr. Sammy Joseph – at least quarterly.

- Issue you an official partner certificate.

- Offer you from time to time, special, discounted gifts for your spiritual growth and upliftment through our website, programs and outreaches.

\Your commitment is to:

- Pray for us always.

- Be committed to support our broadcasts, meetings and outreaches in your area.

- Support us financially with your monthly 'seed' as said in Philippians 4:17.
- Always speak positive words of affirmation on the ministry, Dr. Joseph – and his family.

If you would love:

- Host the *International Experience Harvestways Conference* in your country / region;
- Become a vision partner / supporter of *Sammy Joseph Ministries*; or
- Become a volunteer at any of our outreaches.

Please write:
Sammy Joseph Ministries
P.O. Box 15129
Birmingham
West Midlands, England
B45 5DJ
admin@harvestways.org
Call: (+44) 7758195466 / 7854675159
Visit our website: www.harvestways.org

THANK YOU!

Contact Addresses
In the United Kingdom & Europe
Pulse Publishing House
Sammy Joseph Ministries
Box 15129
Birmingham, England
West Midlands, U.K
B45 5DJ
Tel: *(+44) 7758195466 / 7854675159*
pulsepublishinghouse@harvestways.org

In Nigeria, West Africa
Pulse Publishing House
1 Harvest Way, Off Elewura Street
Behind Zartech / GLO Office,
Off Elewura Street
Challenge, Ibadan,
Nigeria, West Africa.
pulsepublishinghouse@harvestways.org

LISTEN & **SUBSCRIBE** to *'Harvestways With Sammy Joseph'*
broadcast on the Youtube

HarvestWays is the official 'GoodNews-teller-ministry' of
Sammy Joseph Ministries. At HarvestWays Media, we aim to
broadcast - on the internet, radio, the social media and the
TV - informative programing and teachings offering relevant
solutions to relevant issues based upon the Word of God!
Subscribe today - and help us spread the Word!

Comments or Contact us:
Box 15129, Birmingham, England B45 5DJ.
Telephone: (+44) 7758195466 OR Text: 7854675159
admin@harvestways.org

You may also follow *Sammy Joseph Ministries* on the facebook at *facebook.com/SammyOJoseph*

Also present on *Twitter, Instagram, Facebook & Periscope* as *"@SammyOJoseph"* Make sure you follow him – even as he follows our Lord Jesus Christ!